ARIADNE'S ISLAND

The Miami University Press Poetry Series
General Editor: James Reiss

The Bridge of Sighs, Steve Orlen
People Live, They Have Lives, Hugh Seidman
This Perfect Life, Kate Knapp Johnson
The Dirt, Nance Van Winckel
Moon Go Away, I Don't Love You No More, Jim Simmerman
Selected Poems: 1965-1995, Hugh Seidman
Neither World, Ralph Angel
Now, Judith Baumel
Long Distance, Aleda Shirley
What Wind Will Do, Debra Bruce
Kisses, Steve Orlen
Brilliant Windows, Larry Kramer
After a Spell, Nance Van Winckel
Kingdom Come, Jim Simmerman
Dark Summer, Molly Bendall
The Disappearing Town, John Drury
Wind Somewhere, and Shade, Kate Knapp Johnson
The Printer's Error, Aaron Fogel
Gender Studies, Jeffrey Skinner
Ariadne's Island, Molly Bendall

ARIADNE'S ISLAND

MOLLY BENDALL

Miami University Press
Oxford, Ohio

Library of Congress Cataloging-in-Publication Data

Bendall, Molly.
  Ariadne's Island / Molly Bendall.
    p. cm.
    ISBN 1-881163-39-3 (cloth : alk.paper) -- ISBN 1-881163-40-7 (pbk. : alk. paper)
    I. Title.

PS3552.E5384 A89 2002
811',54--dc21   2001030927

The paper in this book meets the guidelines
for permanence and durability of the Committee
on Production Guidelines for Book Longevity
of the Council on Library Resources. ∞

Printed in the U.S.A.

9 8 7 6 5 4 3 2 1

For Vivienne

CONTENTS

Ariadne doesn't yet believe, quite
*   she is witnessing what her eyes see--*
she's only just woken from a trap
(of sleep)
*   found herself alone on the island.*
And Theseus, heedless as storm & wind
*   carves up the waves as he goes*
and throws their love-words overboard.

Catullus

SAIL

The trick is the flow. Little fish with storms on their minds.
          Stones don't reveal

what they covet today, but I know them.

          I gather scraps and throw them back,
throw them back to the waves
                    even as they climb toward my room.

                    So where to go when my pockets are light?

          Night-shy, evening shells–
          all eyelids and ears.

The glinting blades and their kindred–do they ever say,
          no one ever, clean start, and
     clean, stark, smoothed galleries within galleries
     I want
emptied of desire, but geled with color and domes of sea-
sweets.

                    Look at the lapses in between stars,
                    vertebrae washed up at my feet.

OVER SLEEP

The long reason of his life pours out–
slender-drool-string. But I've built

this canopy. Yes, the

shipwrecked girl left for dead.

Not as haunted as you'd like to think. Lone tribeswoman?
                    Leader of an expedition?

                    And I'm nudged by
        the tumbles of sand.
                            I was meant to appear.

Cannibal, well, yes. That's how I get closer,
                    just believing
it. I have plates and knives, and, oh yeah, I have

moods–out here anything can lead me astray.

GLEAM

The silver and the undead haven't peeled out yet.
    Even the cats have declined to inhabit this island.

"I promise you," he said, "I'll make my way through Svengalis

and the whips and come back to you."
 Well, nothing's as easy
                as you think. I'll sit

on this rump of sand I've made, under my frond umbrella.

Hey boy, more margaritas please. Then I'd say,
oh you don't have to. Sit down, have some–

don't listen to me–

        Desertion has made me irritable.

        The inlets are my arenas.
I'm listening to the qualities of fish-voices, many dimensional,

drumming. They gleam in the low tide as the sun

keeps pieces of my skin. The birds

        touch my elbows. O darkest

bird, nearly purply black. You, pirate,
                come closer. I've reserved
                your space.

SILK THREADS

What gloss is this–sweat-sheen, fruit pulp?
There's a house of shimmering water,
a guest-house
alive with eyes and hoods.
I have to live, being near lips
that never say, the day wanes or the garden's shot.

Beneath I have to watch my feet, careful not
to step near that spindle shell. Its inner

rooms beckon–a swirl and a pleated skirt twists.
I pick up what ought to be my patent leather purse
with no glinting reflection,
only a dark corner, a close shadow.

My treasure map must not have
travelled well.
I might snorkel here, move with
the sea's jellied squares,
float among the blow-up pillows

and poof about as it all yawns and yawns.

BEAST

OK. I'll buy my hallucination. I'll give him a name.

      If he dicks around with my fruit and
my leaves, I'll

think again. He keeps coming out
of a chateau up there.

Way up there. I would rather live in that
cream-stone cave
           even if the floor's cold.

Scandal surrounds the island, bubbling foam-lotion. I can't

ignore his breathing, when the surf's hair is light. And
sometimes he has a bull's head,

grunting, rubbery even,

         and I don't want to kill him, I want
to nuzzle him and lie on top,

rub myself on his head and snout.

Oh Bully, is it your face drawn on the waves?

      Then I could stand it, I could abide the sharp water.

HOLIDAY

        Banishment and exile scent

the water, so I'm wading in a big aperitif.
            It moved me, love-drop, when you
allowed me to help you. The beast was

        quite tame with its little chickory bangs.

Wasn't it a shame I kept thinking of someone else?

You rescued me
too. "Come to my getaway at the shore."

 We threw clothes, appliances in–
pitch it in, smoke it up–

        the ocean's a wince away.
            Couldn't we have summered?

Twice jumbled now, I've cracked the rain
            wide open.

        And near enough but gone.

CIVILIZED

Who was that artist again? What's his
name? I'll look it up

in my library of bark, my bookcase of mud and bricks.
This little hut bulges like a growth. Storms cheat

and snicker. That ridge, it could, it *could* be the Riviera.
                    There's plenty of water and plenty

to want. Unfortunately, I have only one mirror

so I can't see how my hair looks in back. I wake up
and before my eyes open

I swear my piano is sitting there glistening,

                    all its seeds in place.

Screen

The sky's giving me one of
    its tirades again.

I thought I heard gunfire,
        the morse code of an automatic

I heard sometimes in my neighborhood.

Would the shot have stung, burned, like grease-pops?

The jellyfish caught in my bathing suit
top, that sting.

Foaming in, spray, darkening edges. Curling up,

burning. Then blue mixes with liquid gold.
Before the stampede, brutal breathless hooves.

            Angels battered underfoot. If only the leaves
could be helping out, but they're whispering

holding their chins.

    Screen the movie against the white dune,
Master of ceremonies.
            And teach me

to lie down in silver pastures.

CHARMED

Off the ragged hull of
                    a ship a gleam stepped.
A bit of a springy step. It danced on top

of the water. What were my intentions once?

        How I seduced him til we bled.
And found his errand was living-cold but possible.

There I was zipping around, and the gleam wants to show

    me, project a little document on the beach.

            I clip and prune
            the fruit trees,
and I love their tangled breeze.

    Sticky fruit, cut my lip.

    The shore widens and each vow hides another.
And the gleam keeps its shape,

        nearly dark with undertones and skids.

STRANDS OF LIGHT

Out here only the animals

can hate me. The others–professionals, writers,
                    fatherly whim-whams–wish they could

but it's hard to fuck me over if I'm way
out here islanding, thinking

                    of covered wagons and circus

caravans. How they went into inhospitable
        territories.

        The flies flaunt their hunger, the crabs
have too many eyes today.

                Cocksure and thunderous–that's how
he came to me, then I offered my string,

glittery cord, piece of gimp.

I had yet to make it into bracelets and belts

                with gossamer strands flowing out behind.

A FRENZY

Could you hear the hooves kicking
          up dust, matador?

Now they're waiting for me to join them under
the umbrella. I'm living twice, so don't try to guess.

Go on grinding there. It's hotter where you are.

              Satellites are falling into
your oceans. Just try and hide.

Do you miss your nearly-drowned-abandoned-one?

I fill in the dotted lines.
                  I've decked
myself in a nylon scarf. Now I glide
on the incoming tide.

              Your red cape lets me through,
snarling hot air through my nose.
Get ready. Unrolled rugs.

          I can jump through the light–
a pause in the wind.

ASIDE

Make no

mistake.

Some ease

for a sky

alone with

a pressing whisper

that

changes

at will.

And magnified slightly

shines in

the rooms

of

this demi-place.

Soft Color

I go on too long about others–wealthy ones
          charmed ones.

     And I talk with bits of dark

splashing around. I'd say how stunningly detached
she is–her laughter, a single swinging bead on

a cord begs for a silver cage.

          Lamplight accomodates my dance and my

arguments so well. Hibiscus punctuates, gray
               frosty moths repeat like TV fuzz.

I squint hard and still miss the password. I'm like

               one of the conchs out there trying to
match the color of sand. So I spoke into one

I grabbed earlier. Someday they'll all come
               in aromatic robes, silk
sails and new weapons, phones on their belts–

the prophecy I've lived by.

Spumes and Froth

If I seem

too modern, then let me direct you to
            the strident anti-wind that combs

the surfaces backwards and to the desperate
                    veiny channels that I can
        hardly reach.
        Perhaps I'm avoiding some catastrophic misery,

instead of building a temple out here.
            I'm prodding the nervous curtains

                    I've woven from
what's been drowned and rescued.

                I'm sober and need a kiss.
        No fluency–

now doubled over from entertaining.

FRILLS

Cross-hatched, checkered, and blithering–swarms

and swarms of patterns displayed.

                        I'll take a two mile ride
over the white foam.
    I love the undoing, secret agenda

            of the weave. That's when we

                    see the new frontier.
Skather and dreck, Skather and dreck.

So can't I lift the pleasure from there
                        and put it here now,
or adjust it, how?

People wear a tolerant moment, get advice,
move on. Pleasure's outline

            dances a frilly waltz near the cove.

Come on, airy spectators, keep close, the lights aren't

down yet, the trailers haven't started.

FURL

There's more stretch
                in the sky this night.

My shy but pungent snaps of light up there.

Miles from me again, miles from being my crown.
                    And my bed swells
from the heat and floats

                with minor sounds–
    hushes and breaks. Sea anemone come curving
sucking and pouting in elegant

quiet. Diminutive, urgent seduction.

Pinch me awake. Lean me against

the scratchy sage brush. I only *seem* invisible.

MORE SCARABS

Beetles click around
    my trunk of clothes.
        Sometimes the sky's

reflected in their backs.
    It's not so much an answer
as a comeback line, when the birds

rise up from the sharp rock–display, display.

I jump this time, want to insult them for my

reckless moment. In the fretful water,
                a party of old friends...
Until it smooths over.
One thing I don't worry about
                is money, how odd.

He left me with
            shelter and tools. Others come
and talk or I go for a downtown stroll, stop

at a drugstore, apply for a few waitress jobs.

Our few nights together here we spent
                fucking on the sharp sand.

All along he knew he was leaving. The stars were
my enemies. He even laughed when I

feathered his hair. Stars, skittish clover flowers,
I'll come and welcome
            myself on their porches.

INITIATION

Wild sage, greasewood, cacti, cottonwood,
           manzanita, wild cherry.
     My own grotto's here, a cave for hiding

with a shelf for short moments.

      Clear a gate space.
Now to pull the letters up
          from the muck

                  by their stems and hooks.
Squeeze the drifts
  and listen to their drowsy hums.

Latch the trunks and feel the scrapes

of a breeze. Hammer down the rest still
poking up.
            A new nation born,
        the laws nearly uttered.
      Serve them up.
Nibble then dab.

Peaceful is the talking and the occasion makes us ready.

Washed Up

I'm left here with measurements: fingers,
orchestral birds, the null, and

shrill numbing cherubs, leering.

Today the sun shrieked and
              the clouds ruffled uncontrollably.

Lock it up, lock it, the pipers chanted.
Wash tumbled out of the surf unafraid.

              Under a horseshoe crab, under its torture chamber–
dish and dagger–crouches my emptiness.

I've sorted through replicas. I'm
replaying some novel positions and embracing the impossible.

Spread out an *M,* pull it and pull it into a ripple
  a murmur.

ISLAND CALL

No season I've seen. Lightly the algae and I drift.
                We resemble each other.
    Until a flat fish came hovering,

told me to stop behaving like
                        a fugitive.
Note that I'll accept letters in the hollowed out

                        branch near the wing-shaped ledge.
I swear the current changes,
                        pushes its teeth
toward the back of the island, haunting me. Whatever befalls

        me, I'll dance with it, train it
to yearn with me. But I'll dismiss

those who come encumbered with fruits and soothe-talks
                and too many
generous directions.

DELICACIES

Little light species
breezing in their sentiments. Cat-eyed fish, how

theatrical they are–much smooth trembling.
                    Or I've worn these shades too long.

Succulents push up through
the skin here, their martiana green hunkering. Hey you

        round-a-bout angel, lay

down your spectral cape. Need
            a hanger? The air currents,

whipping and resting
        though how awful
            they are.

                They smell

cross and blameful.

Winter wouldn't leave its scent.
            So coy. I'm asking
    "Can't you scream with some conviction?"

    Look, the makeshift chairs,
the ancestors–

they're mouthing the words.

PITCH THIS

Where's my diagram to spiritual
          bliss?
                    Under the roots?

   Mandraked in a big cauldron?

          Coifed in
seaweed? I'd make an easy do-it-yourself video,
if I only had a camera.

     I'll sketch the calm. Beware of the dangers
of scurvy. I think sometimes the surfers

are out there, their black torsos against
          back-tongues of water, weighing the nothingness.
Talk about careers. There are new sounds

from the shallows, teasy pulls from the wind. I'll hold

     a microphone to record

          the splash, the streaks, the smithereens.

CASCADE

What crouches outside my hut
          tonight?
                  Is it he with apologies?
  Or is it another he? I have enough nuts
and dried fish to stay in here for days.

          Stars now, just clicks
in the sky. I let them circle my head, my loose tiara.

     What else can I shop for? I'm kneeling and
something/someone journeys through

        the damp corridors, stops at a figure
on the slippery walls. An upside down message

        curls and uncurls. Someone

feels certain he can come here.
        I know when to leave, when the sky

is ready. —Peel back, let me through.

Mythology Led Me Here

Exploring the jetty. It lengthens out a path for me.
Carried a water bottle along.

I like the way the view is a green
                    valley of pleasantness.

    I recollect some early time and whisper
proverbs, fan myself with leaves.

        So spiced I could nearly sweep clear
    the rattling.

                And I prefer when the water
resembles
        a countertop. So I leave myself

crockery, serving plates, sheets
of tin—so practical.
                        Then the starfish
tweak me, honestly. Or they shun me.

Aren't they really saying, "Don't shriek,

        be comfortable, welcome oblivion"?

Settlement

Between that palm and that
                    rock lies my generator.

It's made of gaskets, buttons,
   dead prawns, cockle shells. Now fetch me

some friends, or a least a water rug, my diminutive eel.

               Where is my sheltering welkin today?
   Cut off by my makeshift ratty roof
I guess. Can we

make a new one artfully? Sometimes I want
 the gray dusk water spread under

          my backbone, and I
imagine being pushed, revived,
          taken into some invented, but nonetheless

          real, zone of soft
nests and comfy sheets.

ASIDE

Travelling

surface

and bewitching.

A smote or two.

Wither

like a cradle.

The husks

turn sullen

What cause?

No disguising

it.

Vanished

then beckoned

by degrees.

Mix

The gnarly bendable bark
works best
for molding my most desirous mooncalf.

Belly-sugar, I've made you boiling and bursting with
covetous charm.

Out here the boats have all blown, blown, blown away–
blew with salt comforters.

And the sideways skiffs I pocket up.
Seldom do I need to

draw from my reserve.

Let it be strange.
Let only the stars weigh on my shoulders.
And butter the crust–it can
act as a salve.
Then I calm him–my softly, my dirty work.

More Delicacies

They tell me. They–the periwinkles, the mussels–
            tell me even families betray you,
      bring you back to zeroes
and strip

            the feathers from trees.
      Desertion lies there in a pretty way
like a skin casing or a torn jellyfish–

            prism of purples surrounded
by lacy buttons.

When more wash up to my feet,
                        I clench for a minute,
then keep
      walking over them. I adjust and wait

for the tall birds sporting
                  their phantom attire
            to poke around and
      tear with their beaks.

HUNT

That's skill—
              she just stands (never mind her
posture), holds up the spear and throws.
              She's my idol, and all the gingery

seconds hold their breaths. Soon graciousness will

                          abound. I'll lure
          the lions, look in their candyish mouths.
      The wake of your

leaving will disperse, then I'll move in
    for the kill.
        Still, she quakes when those knives
                          come right through the air
              and shine gallantly, alluringly.

Neither the giants
                      nor the ruffians that hover around
      offer any solutions
                      this salty day.

SHIVER

She lifted the O's
of her sleeves, that starlet angel.
And the space has a lofty scent though it's smeared now

across the air.
I've seen how my limbs go on living

by themselves, trying to be kissed. Feather-skinny

lines of light rub against
my blood.
If only I could keep dressing in exits,

then questions

and gaps would stay in fashion.

Sage brush catches a threat
then drags me down shivering. A willow dress would

have more wrap-around shadows and cling.

Sleek blue-bellied gulls, bring on the sneers.

The other faces
I knew
were so late with their shade.

Storm Slides

Spasmodic lightning's so crucial
    in reminding me of drama out here,
      of the nerves

that make up the sky. Wide awake ocean,

   you're balded by the flash. Nope, not
  an inch of privacy for you this evening.

I want
   to tend to you, all your hidden
dinnerware and china cups. Then I could zoom over

to the resort skimming the tarnished lid
    of you,

 and visit the retired character actors.
    They snap their fins on, why not?

Cajole me, sip some.
    Commas of silver cells up close.

AUDITION

A shiver and an eyebrow arch she had.
        And the dibbley-dab and the run-with-it.

Only her calves moved, her thighs trapped in the skirt.

    Above, clouds crowd, men hover, her chorus.
                Far beneath that filmy wave, let's talk.

I've got a riddle for you dreamboat–my hair's all moon.

        I sing with two hands on a knee. Shhh...pink and black.

Haven't found the drift here, but some old skins
                make a shoulder cape.
Sharp, tiny bones wash up and pull the sand.
                        Minor bites to tend to.

An ankle scrape, then a smear.

Popping seeds and running down the velvety aisles.
            My theatre–a run-down mosque–still attracts
a crowd. Push and pull that kelp.

Luff Luff.
        In this new candlelit era I've heard so many
rumors under the sudsy water.
                Bubble shum. Currents.

Wading through the languid shine
                so I approximate my entrance.
    Veins have been embroidered on the glassy vinyl sheet.

    What can I burn in time for this harvest?

Wing Shows

Something scuds away from
     my edgy island before I'm awake.
Has he come again with his dark moves?

         Perhaps he's left Tobacco in a box.
I've already dealt with monsters
and ogres and their beards.

         How quiet he must have been leaving.
Quietness aloft, quietude abounds.

  Add it to my checklist–Can I use this rusty sword?
How about this tossed over crate? He had to toss cargo

     to move so fast across the shine.

City noise lured him, its helicopters and radio snarl.
     I have them,
my own disturbances. We get on our riot gear, bull horning,
  "Move away from the building."

Lunching below the sun-scrape, I bid that body new flow.

What whirls around
        when privacy is needed?

Beasts of Air

Wing-spreads, full as iron.

        I've withheld my fangs and any devouring tendency.

I love how they flood the air
        then float to kiss with a flaming feather.
They're heavy-footed though as they bear down

                        in their tangles of color.

I could have parted my lips.

                I'm still buttoned up. I can't trust me
any longer. There's no more looking from the outside.

In their sparky processions they clash and moan.
                I'll probably imitate their dip-turns later
        in my new number: Pain and Departure.

        Bold chirping presides royally in the throngs
of their folderol.

        I conjure
                and conjure and still I'm undiscovered.

STITCHES

I think the man I didn't give change to
                    lurks around my cruising rock.

Although I'm shucking and peeling–so busy,
  there's no plot to untangle
from the scratchy earth.
                    Nuts in between the lines of heaven.

Urchins parade the whole month around, and
new months I've taken to measuring in loaves.

Steeped in gray
  the hill's muscles overheat.
Rolls of glitter, spools of light.

Who's near the noise I knew?
                    Bones are for needles,
  sticks are to chew, and with my scallop brooch,

I'm aloft and singing.

Odds eddy in lame laps.
                    And I shelve them all as
I cut smoothly the vacancies here.

GLARE

I've come down with moon-blink tonight
                    and have nothing for it

but a psalm and a strong stitch. My soft

        rock wall needs panelling for
me to lean on.
                As usual I can't afford it.

    My autoharp strings could accompany
        something of this
                            new light
and the echo trapped inside a shell.

            The fairies have perched and purled
    in their nests. Blue Monday is here.
So I'll drape my cathedral too in blue.

    Monday and its night-rule called to startle
or strike   no difference where.

Then there was the fairies' special way of bristling
                and flying back and forth
festooning with blue,

                    making nights into patterns,

stitchery I'm blinded by.

HAZE AND DECOR

A night following a night–
                if I blow on the saved-up

embers under the ash, I can start a new blaze.
  Oh the pleasures of do-ing, and my

          shish kebobs heat up. After they've
sublimed to a cool exhale,

I send up some twinkles inside this proscenium.

The sky spreads its thick net of stars. No sleep
           then waiting.
Pillow me more, soft light. That's nearly all
       to wish for.

   And I've outgrown a lot.
My songs now sparking open and shut like dragonflies.

        Out of their deep the devilfish chant
with me roiled and dapper. And eyes–such shimmering

   in their swollen approach.

*A*SIDE

Caught

now

by its flicker.

Hyphen

uniting phantoms.

Before

the lapse

of gray smoke

swerves up

and

   gone.

So it's

insinuated

not heard, not

dreamt.

REFLECTION

These animals whose faces are wider than planets

will never change back into men.

I'm sure the centaurs from the yellow forests would be
a comfort should they come for a short while.

Jellyfish sun in their petticoats.
Ghosts smooth down in the spindrift.

Stones fall from a ledge into thunder,
tired of their own voices.
Patterns of scales

on a washed-up fish make a map of a Byzantine city—
interlocking S streets, mazes without keys.

No axis, only swirls by which to measure the time
before the what-I-know-now.

Out of clay I shape a bowl
like a pelican's mouth and press in chips
of blue shell for sequin shine.

What shall I lust after now?

A lobster whose claws turned into paws
and then crept up for company?
Or the face of a knight pulled from a squid?

THIN AIR

An anemone
                comes a little furtively,
                          only slightly–it waits to be drawn.
     It bobs then makes a tunnel, a coil of knotty blue.

                I draw it curl by curl
not to forsake its curtainy breeze. A dab of red, a blister

     of white, and with a lip-touch, I've made it–another.

My laundry hovers in the sky, rinsed. In another place
          even more far flung, I'll remember

                          this as carefree–lit windows,
white columns. Even with raw skin under it all,
     I can't be pushed too far.
                Hills in showcase-green, leaves rustling.

          The wind tells all

when the forest is forbidden to tell.

Drift and Release

Just when I needed
          a page to sleep by,

 I saw clear water curling
                    out of the ground and
found a narrow canal–drops, clarity,
                              smooth sailing.
The cups and boats I made have bark pulled so tight
     and more silver clay to fill in the holes.

 Let the falling spring scroll down
                the ridge.
                         Waterways of mine and lostness.
Sing to them–
          someday you'll know,

     you above the ridge, unremarkably folded,
nearly captive.
          Lean and rest nearby. I've drawn this Book of Colors.

     Acquaint yourself with the impulse of the slant.
  The double moonrises that someone had
                    surely touched

  are now abandoned to the shine sca-money.

Shelf

If I could
          borrow those pearl-lined compartments,

                    shelve some spices in my New World
     then I'd

look at snips and tiny books with mirror pages.

     I've hung scallops with knuckles
                         all in the old-white of napkins,
lamps.
          Wasn't it certain?

                    Waves boil under the floating houses.
Now as the nests drift and tug on the undone sheets and
     the haze
                         is driven off, my empty wings revive

to the flash of the flying fish—my Saturns, my Jupiters,

and I, for you, am slow and sure
                                   sweeter than light

     fooled by nerves   by animals lifting.

Riddle Me

What complaints I've given
            this storm of birds.
                        Then it
            becomes the hour to
        recite my repetitions, slipping and dragging
        near the gloved light.

    Riddle me, riddle me.
                Soon dark will haul me forward.
        Still blue–
            my glide across the air,
                    my quick darling
(and I wish I had amnesia).
                    These wave-glossed
            spirals   balustrades

in their odd whites,

    and the rounded sky–it does
            harm so poignantly.

    And harpstrings that lie on this shell
                            are directions for building.
            Oh, only to be accomodated. This story hangs

                near me, suspended above the water,
hangs by ribbons and by troubles.

Marching High Up

The parrots must have
        flown
     from the mainland.
               High in their greens–and
I'd desire nothing. The accompaniest pauses for me
       until I dance
   or scurry with animals around me.

Messages on the leaves have walled me in.
       On the isle be great hills of gold
that pismires keep
 full diligently.

        Hungering for a new treat,
   mellow and syrupy.

     And there groweth
a manner of fruit as though it were
        gourds. And when they be ripe, men
cut them atwo, and men find within

     a little beast, in flesh,
  in bone, and blood,
      as though it
were a little lamb without wool.

Close to their preening I stayed. Beyond them,
   the frail cargo, a bushel in a vapor.

      And I've turned in my sleep
          to my sleep.

ZENITH

          A stroke on no page, only a give
on the surface.
               Not to be stroked in this shadow-line
and not to be said. Never, never.
  No talk. Except for this–

  See the arrow I've made,
              and the cautions I've spent.
                              I gather my
oval dishes, awash, then dotted with letters. I'm sheltered
  and fixed now.
            Look, my silver pattern I've inherited from
              fish-scales and sunlight.

Only to show near the River of Inclination.

  Now that's like it. Not too frantic.

This platter smoothed from waves with a wisp
    and curl of herbs.
                  Tender meat on it

          and a galaxy fingered lightly.
  I write here in my Handbook of Everyday Magic.
            I press another leaf,

ink it and the veins give it away.

GREEN LEAVES

Luster me into forgiveness
                    soft green light.
Emerald birds, your patterns
                    incline over the pitched-up coverlets.
And bean-size clams meadow my view—

they show their tufts and star-shoots
                    as they tongue down into their burrows.

I don't recognize this, but it's all I know to do.

Interior decorating becomes me

with bundles and sharp forces. Those heart cockles,
cupped and crenellated, more than ready

                    for my low table done in chartreuse
                    or tropical teal.
                    Are they mine? These ornamented trees?

Calendar

My bashful weather,
you seem higher. And rolls and wash of turbulence–

sequined sardines below.
May your boat always be falling near the edge, teetering.

I've been dirtier than this.
When an old day was twisted in its tense.

The surfaces disarm me, weightless and silky
as they do.

I wait for a branch to snap. Stall.
My limbs hang separately,
my feet, scarred tapestries.

What may be falling into the vast pile?

Does it make your fetid heart stir some?

There was glitter around the cove. (Oh, I
overreach again.)
Day brought on an arraignment of white sun,

not a moment really, but there's an apprehension of
the next–what–?
A curled arm coming
up from the sand?

AT THE CRUX

Grieving takes its lyric turns,
anciently,
sometimes *en pointe.*

Among all this business,
a flavor has no body.
Then I bask
with my sea-faced lovers. They say,

"Look into the camera, state your name."
So I'll slice down a spine, blow through a bone.

One wrong fin slaps the water.
And it's the afternoon ache,
when the rain's in pieces.
Remember the old sound?

A word with you, I call to the black curtain.

I might row out later
after wiping the table dark.
I'm framed in oval and my likeness shows a gash,
sinew eeking out.

Size would care if I took a needle to it.
And if the horses would hurry down the path,
I'd hang bells on their giving necks.

DISCLOSURE

I listen for the fur-dreams...

            I want them back–too lovely
        too lovely–.
                        It's when
    I come lip to lip with him and
                        nod closely into the divide
that never was.

            I'll create a star-sighting–
        lots of hubbub and nudging. Another late, late enter-
prise.

            No one sees beyond the minnow sparks.
    Icy rims pool and pool, jading me a palace.

                There's a charge for
            the sleepwalker who leaves

            a bite, a dotted crescent.
        Then bellows.

MIDNIGHT TERRITORY

Uncharted   ill-behaved
      space I've pieced together.

Slag this and nod here with patience
      for the rest of the somewhat-night.

      Chills come through at suspicious angles and
shiver me into cold blueness. Wings lost in a
    reflection
      in a wilderness of tentacles and curls.

What I most cherish here are the white
      mariposa blossoms (at least they're white with some
doubt on my Land of No Return)–paper shells,

      memos reporting on what buoyancy is left.

      Soon, my pillow's full of writing.
I'll chew on this late and

        whisper it at another speed.

Fallen

Go pluming small feathers.

And all the sister waves flutter soft away.

Stretching stems across a frame, I weave them,
make them skins.
                    Another body comes forward–one
from dream, sliding, taking shape.

So come, abide in this chink, as if it were grace-sleep.

The jimson weed and evergreens couldn't be
                    more conspicuous.
Blow here, my wish-callers. Start lightly,
wash over my lap.

                    How will I look with fins and a fluke?
The wind falls

from its heights and sighs
                    against the fishy glances.

ALMS

No mourning now, no looking from
                    without,
        though I read minds shamelessly.

These flowering ultimatums
                        I invent for myself.
                I can lug around the excess sky, and a few
        gilded moons fall from the cracks.

    I'd gotten
                wind of places like this.

                            But say what you want
wild lilies. Whales, tilt on, knife up from the beams.
    Tall grasses need
            a passing phrase.

        Shells flash and turn in the rough air
after I string them.
                        Only gulls fly darkly through the
        corridors,
                pulsing like my blood, sea-surge.

VANQUISH

I climbed

to the platform of static,
                    checked out fringes and moss.

        I could view this sunroom as a luxury,
            find the right architect who'd see
its flesh and admire

                my shape alongside.
    Sometimes I'll just move in slow
                            motion
        to see how the glow reacts, what the grass withholds.

That's the plum of loneliness. And deep
in my lungs fruits ripen, a low murmur begins.

    Nothing compares to
                    the thistles' hair,
            its deadliness, its lure.

    I thought I'd use the urchin as a dial,
                    make it click.
I should be more delicate,
                but who's watching? I scissor the glass
surface, the edges curl up in reaction, arousal.

Bubbles cluster in a lather of air-rooms
            and blossoms.

EDGE

A charm to say, a remnant to press.
And what grows over my head–
a sorrow-roof.
I was a gray girl ash-haired, elegant
and a singular
warrior at the same time.

I'll stay in the way of questions. If only I had
an aerial view of the island. It would have
the busy detailing of a watch.

No one risks
the ropes like me. The moth ate songs–
wolfed words.
Replies are sent in envelopes fastened with coral and twine.

Then strands and strands of weed.
I was nearly taken
in by a snail.
Narrowly I stand in this hallway,
my cape of cormorant feathers tilts

and shines on the lift.

STING

Squeeze me a long look.
    The dunes taunt with shadow.

              Heckling gulls make me thirsty and sore.

        I tried the ones with nectar.
       What delight it was–sucking the animal right out
               of its shell.

  Fang me little serpent.
        Beetles click. Those nerves they hide.

I've taken to scraping the fruit, using them for spice. I've
created zest! Let's purr over it.
          Then the planting, indentations, the rows
     for seed pods, wanting-sighs, little teasers.
        Can't pick you yet. Drowse then.

Can you unhinge the slack
 long enough for me to stop whining?

             I like to wash out and
swell and gain a step going in.

INCLINATION

   Time to summon those
metal fasteners.   Time to watch the moon-eggs

      roll and fix themselves.
Can't you tell I've been celibate for–what's it been?–
                washes and leaves of days,
   except for the occasional sharpness
                        with a pelican friend.
In horizontal mist I tell him
                        show off your slips and stays.
      Like once
she loved that bull, all its wiry hair.

   Time to weave
                the diving fins   a silver stitch
   pull   shore up
then shallow   over shimmer   leap   and pour

            I'm pulled into petals and I'm surprised

I welcome it so.

NOTES

Travels, Sir John Mandeville (c.1356). From the 1725
Cotton Manuscript.

A Feast of Creatures, (Selections from the Exeter book of
Anglo-Saxon Riddle-Songs) translated by Craig Williamson,
1982.

The Poems of Catullus, translated by Peter Whigham, 1966.

Acknowledgments

American Poetry Review: "Gleam," "Beast," "Screen," "Strands of Light," "A Frenzy," "Spumes and Froth," "Delicacies," "Pitch This"

Colorado Review: "Drift and Release," "Alms"

Denver Quarterly: "Shiver," "Mythology Led Me Here," "Zenith"

Kestral: "Silk threads," "More Scarabs," "Soft Color"

The New Republic: "Reflection"

Painted Bride Quarterly: "Over Sleep," "Charmed," "Island Call," "Stitches"

Paris Review: "At the Crux," "Thin Air"

Tin House: "Cascade," "Storm Slides"

Tri-Quarterly Review: "Frills," "Calendar," "Fallen," "Vanquish," "Inclination"

Volt: "Audition"

Yale Review: "More Delicacies"

Molly Bendall was born in Richmond, Virginia. Her first book of poems *After Estrangement* won the Peregrine Smith Poetry Prize in 1992. Her second book *Dark Summer* was published in 1999 by Miami University Press. She has received the Eunice Tietjens Prize from *Poetry* magazine, the Lynda Hull Poetry Award from *Denver Quarterly,* and two Pushcart Prizes. She currently teaches at the University of Southern California and lives in Venice, California.